LADYBIRD  HISTORIES

The Vikings

History consultant: Philip Parker, historian and author
Map illustrator: Martin Sanders

A catalogue record for this book is available from the British Library

Published by Ladybird Books Ltd
80 Strand, London, WC2R 0RL
A Penguin Company

001

© LADYBIRD BOOKS LTD MMXIV

LADYBIRD and the device of a Ladybird are trademarks of Ladybird Books Ltd.

ISBN: 978-0-72328-841-1
Printed in China

The Vikings

Written by Jane Bingham
Main illustrations by Seb Camagajevac
Cartoon illustrations by Peter Lubach

Contents

Who Were the Vikings?

Most people think of the Vikings as raiders. They picture armed warriors seizing treasure, killing innocent people and setting fire to homes. But this is only part of the picture. Between the 700s CE and the 1000s CE, the Vikings created a rich civilization that has influenced the way we live today.

People of the north

The Vikings lived in Scandinavia, in lands that are now Denmark, Sweden and Norway. In their Scandinavian homelands, they survived by farming, hunting and fishing. Some Vikings were craftspeople, who worked with metal, wood, leather and bone. Some were merchants, who sailed long distances to exchange their goods.

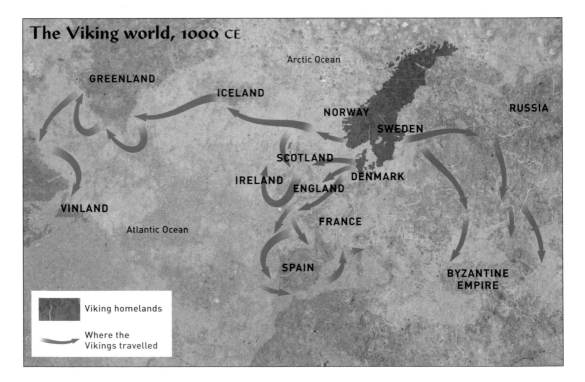

The Viking world, 1000 CE

Arctic Ocean

GREENLAND

ICELAND

NORWAY

RUSSIA

SWEDEN

SCOTLAND

IRELAND   DENMARK

ENGLAND

VINLAND

FRANCE

Atlantic Ocean

SPAIN

BYZANTINE
EMPIRE

Viking homelands

Where the
Vikings travelled

Raiders

There were several reasons why the Vikings left their homelands and began raiding: there were too many people for the farmland to support; the overpowering control of the kings made people want to leave; and the wealth of foreign towns and monasteries attracted warriors to set out on raids to conquer them.

How do we know?

The Vikings did not keep written records, but we do have evidence to show how they lived. Archaeologists have uncovered homes, ships and forts, and have found objects, such as weapons, jewellery and coins. Some poems and stories were written down at the end of the Viking age. Historians have also been able to study vivid accounts by people in countries attacked by Vikings.

Settlers

Once warrior leaders had seized a foreign territory, boatloads of settlers arrived to set up communities. By the 1000s CE, there were Viking settlements in Britain, France and Russia. Some people settled in Iceland and Greenland, and a few daring Vikings even travelled to North America (Vinland)!

Viking communities relied on fishing and farming to feed their people.

Viking Society

The society that gave rise to the Vikings was already established in Scandinavia by the 700s CE. These people spoke a language called Old Norse and lived in tribes ruled by local chieftains. Gradually, three main groups developed – these were the jarls, the karls and the thralls. In the early Viking age, the jarls were very powerful, but by the end of the 900s CE Denmark, Norway and Sweden each had their own king and the jarls had lost much of their power.

Jarls

The jarls were warrior lords who owned large areas of land. They lived in big houses and held lively feasts for their local community. Each jarl had a band of warriors whom he could summon to defend his land. If the jarl decided to raid foreign countries, warriors would join his raiding party.

Karls

The karls, or freemen, were the biggest group in Viking society. Most of the karls were farmers, but some had other skills and worked as craftspeople or traders. As well as farming, the karls trained to be warriors. They were ready to fight whenever they were needed.

Thralls

Thralls were slaves. They were usually foreigners who had been captured during Viking raids. Most thralls worked on farms or as servants in wealthy homes. They had very few rights and they could be bought and sold by their masters. A few thralls saved enough money to buy their freedom.

Things and kings

The Vikings held large open-air meetings, called Things. People gathered at their local Thing to discuss their laws, sort out any problems and punish criminals. Things were run by the local jarl, and all the karls could attend the meeting and join in the discussions.

By the end of the Viking age, Things were no longer needed and most had died out. Instead, the kings decided how to run their countries.

A mysterious name

Nobody knows how the Vikings got their name, but some experts believe it came from the word 'Vik' meaning a bay, or from 'Viken' – a region in Norway.

Members of the community gathered to discuss local matters at a Thing.

Farming, Hunting and Fishing

Some parts of the Viking homelands were not very good for farming, but people did their best to live off the land. When they were not busy farming, men went hunting and fishing to find extra food for their families.

Farming

Farmers had oats, barley or rye in their fields. They also grew vegetables, such as cabbages, beans, turnips and carrots. Cows, sheep, pigs, goats and chickens were kept on Viking farms. Wool from the sheep was woven into cloth. Milk from the cows, sheep and goats was made into cheese and butter.

Men, women and children worked on farms.

Hunting

People relied on hunting for some of their food, especially in the winter months when stocks were low. Men set out in groups, armed with spears and bows and arrows. They hunted large animals, such as reindeer, wild boar and bears, as well as smaller creatures, like foxes and rabbits. Hunters tracked down wild geese and ducks, and some even climbed cliffs to capture seabirds. The animals they caught produced useful meat, leather and fur. The birds' soft feathers were often used as padding for winter coats and quilts.

A farmer's year

In the springtime, farmers were busy sowing crops. In summer, there was not as much work to do, so the Vikings could go raiding. In the autumn, they gathered in the harvest. In the winter, it was too cold for raiding so the farmers went hunting.

Fishing

The Vikings caught and ate a lot of fish. They used traps, nets and spears to catch herring, salmon and cod. People who lived on the coast hunted seals, walruses and even whales. Back at home, the fish were hung out to dry so they would last for months.

Viking Homes

Viking homes were busy, crowded places, with parents, children and grandparents all sharing the same house. Most houses were rectangular with high, sloping roofs. Inside was a single room where all the family ate, worked and slept. These long, rectangular homes are generally known as longhouses.

At the centre of the house was the hearth. This was a large stone fireplace with an iron cauldron hanging over it. The cauldron was used for cooking and heating water, and the fire was kept burning all the time to give heat and light. Some smoke escaped through a hole in the roof, but most of it stayed inside, making the house very smoky.

Building materials

Homes were often made from wood, but not everyone could afford a wooden house. Poor people built their homes from a mixture of mud and sticks, called wattle and daub. Roofs were usually thatched with straw or reeds, or covered with wooden tiles. In Iceland, where wood was scarce, people built their homes from stones and grassy turf.

This longhouse has been cut away to show the inside.

Furniture

Viking homes did not contain much furniture. Some families had a wooden table, but only the rich had chairs and beds. Instead, people sat on benches along the walls. At night, blankets and furs were spread over the benches to turn them into beds. Tools were hung from pegs or ropes, and any valuables were stored in wooden chests.

A special seat

At the centre of the community was the jarl's house, which had a feasting hall decorated with tapestries and carvings on the walls. The jarl's High Seat was carved from wood with pillars that could be removed. Viking settlers often took these pillars with them to new lands.

Food and Feasting

The Vikings ate two main meals a day – one in the morning and one in the evening. Most people ate off wooden plates and drank from wooden cups, but some wealthy families used pottery dishes. Meat was cut up with a knife, but most of the time people used their fingers to eat, and scooped up any liquid with a hunk of bread.

Wealthy Vikings had a healthy, varied diet. They ate plenty of fruit and vegetables, as well as milk, cheese and eggs and a range of meat and fish. Meat was usually cooked in a stew with vegetables and herbs. Poorer people survived mainly on bread and porridge. Most families ate barley bread, but the rich had loaves made from wheat flour.

The most common drink was ale, which was made from barley, but people also enjoyed a sweet drink called mead, made from honey, water and yeast. Wealthy Vikings drank wine imported from France and Germany.

Viking feasts

Kings and jarls held feasts to mark special occasions, such as religious festivals, weddings or funerals. Guests sat on benches at long tables covered with dishes of food. Everyone drank large quantities, using drinking horns that were passed along the table. Feasts were lively, noisy events lasting for several days. Some went on for weeks!

Drinking horns

Archaeologists have found several drinking horns in Viking graves. Warriors were buried with their drinking horns so they could continue to enjoy plenty of feasting in the next world!

Entertainers

Guests were entertained very well. Musicians, acrobats and jugglers all performed at feasts, and jesters told jokes and invented silly dances. Poets called skalds recited poems in praise of their host and his ancestors.

Feasts gave people a welcome chance to relax and have fun.

15

Clothes and Jewellery

Men, women and children wore simple clothes made from wool or linen. Clothes were usually woven at home and were coloured with natural dyes made from vegetables and minerals. The Vikings loved bright colours, and their tunics often had a woven coloured border. Wealthy people's clothes were embroidered with expensive gold and silver threads.

Men and boys

Men and boys wore long-sleeved tunics over woollen trousers. The trousers were sometimes bound tightly to their legs with narrow strips of leather. The tunic was fastened with a leather belt, and a purse or knife hung from the belt. In winter, Viking men wore cloaks or furs. The cloak was pinned over one shoulder to keep the sword arm free at all times.

Boys wore smaller versions of men's clothes.

Beards and plaits

It was fashionable for Viking men to plait their beards into interesting shapes. This looked good, and also stopped their beards from blowing in their faces! Some men also plaited their hair, and some wore a headband to keep their hair in place.

Women and girls

Women and girls wore a long under-dress, covered by a tunic. The tunic straps were fastened by a pair of brooches linked by chains. Some women attached useful objects to these chains, such as a knife, a key or a comb. In winter, women wore cloaks round their shoulders, fastened at the neck with a heavy brooch.

Women and girls wore warm, loose-fitting clothes.

Jewellery

Vikings loved jewellery. Men and women wore brooches, rings and arm-bands. Women had strings of beads, and even children had lucky charms hanging round their necks. The rich wore delicate jewellery made from gold and silver, while the poor used bronze, pewter, glass and bone to make their necklaces, brooches, rings and charms.

box brooch

arm-band

cloak pin

tunic brooch

ring

Viking Crafts

In the early Viking age, most people lived in isolated communities. This meant they had to make everything they needed. Some people became extremely skilled at a craft and passed on their talents to the next generation.

In the later Viking period, there were many specialist craftworkers. Some set up workshops in towns and some travelled from farm to farm selling their wares.

Working with wood

Viking carpenters built sturdy homes and ships, as well as simple furniture and chests. They knew which timbers to use for each job and decorated their work with delicate carvings.

A pole-lathe was used to produce bowls, plates and cups. A wheel attached to a foot pedal shaped the wood into different objects.

A good comb
Antlers, tusks and animal bones were carved into delicate objects, such as buckles and combs. One worker who used bone was very proud of his craft. His comb bears the inscription: 'Thorfast made a good comb.'

Working with metal and leather

Blacksmiths made a range of useful objects, from cooking pots and tools to keys and locks. Specialist metalworkers produced fine weapons, helmets and jewellery. Leatherworkers made shoes and belts, sheaths for knives and quivers for arrows. They also made strong helmets and jackets to protect warriors in battle.

leather purses

keys

metal helmet

Weaving cloth

Viking women made all their family's clothes and blankets. Some talented women created colourful tapestries for the walls of their homes. First, they dyed and spun the wool. Then, they used a loom to weave the thread into cloth. The family loom was kept inside the home, so the women and girls could carry on with their weaving whenever they had time.

Viking looms had long vertical threads, which were held down with heavy stone rings to keep them straight and tight.

Fun and Games

The Vikings worked very hard, but they also made the most of their leisure time. They enjoyed outdoor sports in all weathers. And when it grew dark, they played games and made music together.

Outdoor sports

In the winter months, the Vikings skated on frozen rivers and lakes. In the warmer weather, they played a game with sticks and a wooden ball, rather like our modern game of hockey. They also raced their boats along rivers and held swimming and diving contests.

The Vikings made skates that they called 'ice legs'. These were leather boots with a carved animal bone tied underneath them.

Indoor games

Board games were very popular. A simple board was scratched on to wood, stone or leather, and bits of bone or pottery were used as counters. In the game of Hnefatafl, one player had a king who could win by escaping to the side of the board. The other had soldiers who tried to surround the king. Some wealthy people played chess, using carved figures made from walrus ivory, bone or amber.

Vikings enjoyed singing and playing music, as well as board games.

Ivory chessmen

A set of ivory chess pieces from Viking times was found in the Scottish Hebrides islands. The pieces are a wonderful example of craftsmanship. They also provide valuable evidence about the way the Vikings looked and dressed.

Writing and Stories

Most Vikings did not know how to write, although they did have a simple alphabet made up of letters called runes. The alphabet was used for carving inscriptions. Runes were carved on memorial stones to kings and warriors. They have also been found on combs, charms and swords. It was believed that the runes gave a sword magical powers in battle.

Runes

Originally, there were twenty-four runes, but by around 700 CE, eight letters had been lost, leaving just sixteen. Runes had straight, simple shapes that could be carved easily. Each rune was a letter, but it also represented a word, such as 'sun' or 'year'. Inscriptions were very hard to read because there were so few letters, and the same rune was used for several different sounds.

f u th a r k h n i a s t b m l R

Carvings of Sigurd

The story of Sigurd the dragon slayer was a popular subject for Viking carvers. The most famous set of carvings was found in a wooden church in Hylestad in Norway. These carvings are now on display at the Museum of Cultural History in Oslo, Norway.

Stories

Because the Vikings had no way of writing their stories down, they learned the tales by heart and passed them on to the next generation. Some of these stories were illustrated by artists in their carvings and paintings.

By the 1100s CE, some Vikings had learned to read and write, and they began to produce records of their stories. The most famous recorder of Viking tales is Snorri Sturluson. He was a poet in Iceland in the 1200s CE. His stories form part of a group of tales known today as the Icelandic Sagas.

Vikings spent the long, dark evenings telling exciting tales of warriors, battles and gods.

Warriors and Raiders

Warriors played an important role in Viking society. In the early Viking age, each jarl had his own band of warriors, who were trained and ready to defend his land or to go on raids to foreign lands. In the later Viking period, kings led well-organized armies into battle. The armies often captured new land for the Vikings in countries such as England and France.

The Vikings usually fought on foot in small groups. They planned their raids carefully and launched surprise attacks on their enemies. Warriors fought fiercely to defend their leader. If he was in danger, they used their shields to make a wall around him.

Viking raiders arriving on the shores of Anglo-Saxon England in 865 CE

Weapons

Most warriors were armed with axes and spears. Some used bows and arrows, and some had lightweight javelins for hurling at the enemy. They carried a circular wooden shield to defend themselves and wore a padded leather jacket. A few of them went bareheaded into battle, but most wore helmets made from leather or metal. Richer, better-equipped Vikings had swords and chainmail tunics.

Berserkers

The berserkers were warriors famous for ferocious fighting. Before a battle, they worked themselves into a frenzy, insulting the enemy and biting their own shields. Berscrkers refused to wear chainmail and howled like wolves as they fought. Some believed that they were protected by magic.

Merchants and Towns

Viking merchants made long journeys to trade with people in distant countries. They returned to their homelands in ships that were laden with precious goods to sell. Foreign merchants also came to the Viking ports to sell their goods and buy Viking products. Some places grew into important trading towns.

The largest Viking towns in Scandinavia were Hedeby in Denmark and Birka in Sweden. There were also thriving towns at York in England and Dublin in Ireland. Viking towns were very busy places. As well as the foreign trade, there was plenty of local business. Farmers came to town to sell their produce and craftworkers displayed and sold their wares.

People came to markets to buy and sell fresh food and hand-made goods.

Foreign trade

The Vikings bought silver, wine, spices and jewellery from foreign merchants. In exchange, they sold furs, leather, iron, timber and ivory made from walrus tusks. Viking merchants also bought and sold slaves wherever they went.

In the early Viking period, there were no coins. Local people simply swapped their goods for something of equal value. Merchants often paid for foreign goods with lumps of silver, known as 'hack silver'. This system continued until the 900s CE, when the Vikings began to make their own coins.

Foreign coins

Coins from Iraq and Syria have been found in Scandinavia. They show that Viking traders had contact with these lands between the 600s and 800s CE.

Women and Children

Some Viking women had a lot of independence, although this depended on their social class. The wife of a jarl or a karl was a respected member of society, but female slaves had no rights at all.

Most women stayed at home. They prepared and cooked the family meals, cared for the children and nursed sick relatives. They also made all the family's clothes and blankets. Wealthy women were helped by slaves, but poorer women did all these jobs themselves.

Women and girls worked in the home.

Work and marriage

A few Viking women did jobs outside the home. Written accounts mention a female skald (poet) and a woman who worked as a carver of runes.

Marriages were usually arranged by a couple's parents, but a Viking wife had the right to divorce her husband if he treated her badly. After a divorce, a wife could keep any property that she had owned before her marriage. Women also played an active part in the way their society was run. The wife of a jarl or karl often advised him on important decisions. She could make decisions if her husband was absent, running the family farm or making trading deals in his place.

Girls and boys

Children did not go to school. Instead, they learned from their parents. Boys learned to hunt and handle weapons. Girls were taught to cook, weave clothes and care for younger children.

Viking Beliefs

In the early Viking age, most Vikings were pagans. This meant they worshipped gods and goddesses and believed in supernatural creatures, such as giants, dwarfs, trolls and dragons. People told many stories about their gods and goddesses. You can read some of these tales on page 33.

Odin

Odin was the ruler of the gods, and the god of war, wisdom and poetry. He lived in Valhalla, the heavenly hall of the warriors. Odin had four companions: two wolves, who fought for him, and two ravens, who brought him news from all over the universe.

Thor

Thor was Odin's son and the god of law and order. He had a magic hammer and was extremely strong. When he rode across the sky, his chariot wheels made the sound of thunder.

Frey

Frey was the god of fertility and birth. The Vikings believed that he made the sun shine and the crops grow, so farmers made sacrifices to him.

Freya

Frey's sister Freya was the goddess of love and death. She rode a chariot drawn by two wild cats.

Worship and sacrifice

People gathered to worship in clearings in the woods. These sacred places were known as groves. They built open-air altars and set up large statues of their gods. Viking ceremonies often lasted for many days and nights, and included human and animal sacrifices. In one ceremony, nine men and nine horses, plus dogs and cockerels were all sacrificed to the gods.

Worship took place in sacred woodland groves.

Viking Legends

The Vikings believed that three worlds made up the universe. These worlds were shaped like dinner plates stacked above each other and were linked by a giant World Tree, called Yggdrasil.

The Viking universe

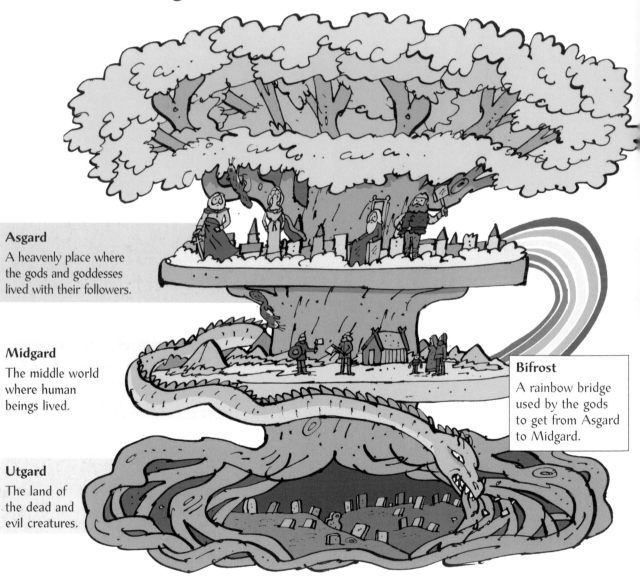

Asgard
A heavenly place where the gods and goddesses lived with their followers.

Midgard
The middle world where human beings lived.

Bifrost
A rainbow bridge used by the gods to get from Asgard to Midgard.

Utgard
The land of the dead and evil creatures.

Thor and the World Serpent

Thor's greatest enemy was the World Serpent that lived in the ocean around Midgard. One day, Thor went out in a fishing boat with a giant as his companion. Thor had an ox's head fixed to his fishing line, and the serpent seized the head in his mouth. Thor was just preparing to kill the serpent with his hammer when the terrified giant cut his fishing line! The World Serpent escaped.

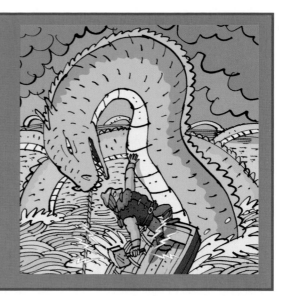

Odin gains knowledge and wisdom

Odin wanted to gain knowledge, so he travelled to Utgard. There he sacrificed an eye in exchange for a drink from the fountain of knowledge. Once he had gained knowledge, Odin longed for wisdom. For nine days and nights he hung from a branch of the World Tree with a spear in his side, learning about the mysteries of death. Then he used his powers to bring himself back to life. Odin used his wisdom to help gods and humans.

The end of the world

The Vikings thought the world would end in an enormous battle, called Ragnarok. At that time, the creatures of Utgard would attack the gods in Asgard, and the people on Midgard would fight each other. After Ragnarok, Midgard would freeze over. Then a new world would be created in which everyone would live in peace.

Death and Burial

The Vikings believed in a world after death. They buried the dead with their possessions, so they would be ready for the next world. Housewives had their jewellery and cooking equipment. Blacksmiths had their tools. Poor people were buried in holes in the ground, marked by a mound of earth. Kings had enormous graves, marked out by memorial stones.

According to Viking beliefs, the dead travelled to different places. Ordinary people went to Hel, which was cold and damp and boring. Very good people went to Asgard, home of the gods. Warriors sailed to Valhalla – Odin's feasting hall, which was part of Asgard. The wicked went to Utgard, a dark and miserable region from which there was no escape.

Ship burials

Some kings were buried in the ground in wooden ships. The ship was packed with weapons and other treasures that the king might need in the next world, and some of his horses and dogs were killed and buried with him, too. Sometimes, a slave girl was killed and laid beside her master so that she could serve him in the next world.

Grave evidence

Archaeologists have uncovered several burial ships. These ships have provided valuable evidence of Viking customs. An Arab traveller, called Ibn Fadlan, witnessed a royal burial in 921 CE. He left a detailed account of what he saw.

In some ceremonies, an entire ship was buried along with possessions in a mound of earth.

35

The Coming of Christianity

The Christian religion came slowly to the Viking homelands. Missionaries began to arrive from other European countries in the 700s CE, but they did not make much progress. It took almost 300 years before all the Viking lands became Christian kingdoms.

Christian rulers

King Harald Blue-Tooth of Denmark was the first important Viking ruler to become a Christian. He was converted around 965 CE, but Christianity did not become widespread in Denmark until the time of Cnut in the 1000s CE. In Norway, two kings, Olaf Tryggvason and Olaf Haraldsson, used violence and threats to force their people to be baptized. Sweden was the last of the Viking homelands to be converted. In 1008 CE, the Swedish king Olof Skotkonung was baptized, but it took another hundred years for Christianity to become established in Sweden.

Hammers and crosses

In some parts of the Viking world, Christianity and the old religion existed side by side. One clever craftsman made two kinds of charms for people to wear round their necks. One charm was shaped like Thor's hammer; the other was in the form of a Christian cross. The metalworker's stone mould has survived, showing his moulds for a hammer and cross side by side.

Changing faith

Once the rulers had abandoned their pagan beliefs, they insisted on dramatic changes. Men, women and children were forced to gather by rivers to be baptized. Statues of gods and goddesses were torn down, and the practice of burying the dead with their possessions was banned. However, some people still continued to worship the Viking gods.

In the 1100s CE, Christian Vikings built wooden churches with steep, pointed roofs. These early churches are known as stave churches. Some of them still survive today.

Ships and Navigation

The Vikings used their knowledge of rivers and seas to design and build all sorts of ships and boats. They included longships for raiding, cargo ships and fishing boats.

Longships

Longships were strong enough to cross stormy seas, and narrow enough to travel down rivers. They were equipped with a sail and many oars, while a steering paddle at the back of the ship controlled its course. Longships had no cabins, so the men simply slept on the deck, ready to start rowing whenever the wind dropped. Most ships had a ferocious-looking beast carved on their prow. They were often known as dragon ships!

The Vikings gave their longships names such as *Seabird* and *Long Serpent*.

Cargo ships

Merchants used cargo ships called knorrs. These were wider and deeper than the longships, and had a large central space where goods could be stored. The knorrs were probably also used for transporting settlers to new lands, along with their possessions and even some animals.

Finding their way

The Vikings had no compasses to help them navigate, but they still managed to cross vast oceans. Sailors relied on the positions of the Sun, Moon and stars to help them chart their course. They also developed a great understanding of waves and sea currents, and studied the habits of seabirds, sea creatures and fish.

The Vikings in England

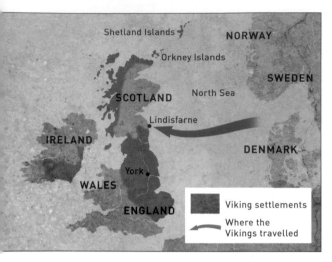

In 793 CE, a band of Viking warriors landed on the island of Lindisfarne, off the north-east coast of England. Lindisfarne was home to a Christian monastery with many fine treasures. The raiders seized the riches and slaughtered many monks before setting off to sea again. The raid on Lindisfarne caused widespread shock and horror. It was the first sign of the terrifying Viking attacks that were to follow across England.

Viking warriors set fire to the buildings and killed many of the monks.

Raiders and settlers

After their first attack, the Vikings raided more monasteries and soon they were launching attacks on the English coast every summer. Then, in the 850s CE, the pattern began to change. Some raiding parties stayed on over the winter, seizing land and building camps.

In 865 CE, Danish ships set out to conquer England. The Danish force became known as the Great Army. First, the Great Army landed in East Anglia, killing many people. Then it spread further. In 866 CE, the Danes captured York. By 869 CE they controlled most of the north-east of England.

The Anglo-Saxons fight back

In 870 CE, the Great Army attacked the kingdom of Wessex in south-western England. Wessex was ruled by Aethelred until his death in 871 CE, when his brother Alfred became king. Alfred gathered an army and began to fight back. After a long and hard campaign, he finally defeated the Danes at the Battle of Edington in 878 CE.

Ragnar Hairy Breeches and sons

According to Viking legend, the Danish invasion of England was sparked off by the death of a powerful chieftain, known as Ragnar Hairy Breeches. The legend says that Ragnar was thrown into a pit of snakes by the king of Northumbria. As an act of revenge, Ragnar's three sons launched their invasion. As well as conquering large parts of England, they captured the king of Northumbria and tortured him until he died.

Ruling England

After his victory over the Danes, King Alfred signed a treaty with the Danish leaders. Alfred ruled western and southern England, but the Danes controlled a very large area in the north and east. This Viking region became known as the Danelaw, and people living there could follow their own Danish laws. Danish rule in the area lasted for almost seventy years, and many Danes settled in England.

Athelstan and the end of the Danelaw

In 927 CE, Alfred's grandson, Athelstan, led the English people against the Danes. He won the Battle of Brunanburh in 937 CE and took control of the Danelaw. Athelstan became the first king of all England. His descendants ruled for the next eighty years, but many Danes still stayed in eastern England.

Aethelred II and the Danegeld

In 978 CE, Aethelred II became the new English king. The Danes soon realized that he was a weak ruler, and they launched new raids on England. Aethelred gathered together a large amount of money, called the Danegeld, which he gave the Danes to make them go away. This worked for a while but the Danes soon returned, asking for more.

By 1002 CE, Aethelred felt the Danes were such a threat that he ordered the killing of all Danish settlers in England. This caused fury in Denmark and led to more violent raids. Finally, in 1013 CE, the Danish king, Sweyn Forkbeard, invaded England. Aethelred fled to France, and the exhausted English people offered Sweyn the English throne.

Sweyn and Cnut – kings of England

Sweyn ruled England for just five weeks before he died suddenly. The throne returned briefly to Aethelred and then to his son. But it was not long before Sweyn's son, Cnut, invaded England and claimed the throne. In 1016 CE, Cnut became king of England and ruled until his death in 1035 CE.

Cnut and the Viking Empire

King Cnut tried to act like an English ruler. He married the widow of King Aethelred, sent home part of the Danish fleet, and used English advisers to help him rule well. During his reign as King of England, Cnut also became King of Denmark, Norway and parts of Sweden. For a brief period in the 1200s CE, England was part of a great Viking empire.

Vikings in the Northern Seas

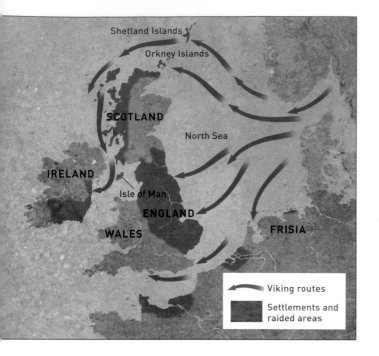

In the late 700s CE, Viking raiding parties sailed west from Norway, looking for new lands to raid and plunder. First, they reached the Shetland Islands. Then they sailed further south and west to other Scottish islands. The raiders used these islands as useful bases to launch attacks on Scotland and Ireland.

Settling in Scotland

Some raiders settled in Scotland, either on the islands or on the coast. They lived as farmers and fishermen in a rocky landscape that was very similar to their homeland. Many settlers married local people and the royal families of Norway and Scotland were joined in 1281 CE when Eric II of Norway married Margaret, daughter of Alexander III of Scotland.

A Viking island

The Isle of Man was a valuable conquest for the Vikings because of its position between the English and Irish coasts. In 1079 CE, a Norwegian chieftain, called Godred Crovan, declared himself ruler of the island, and the Isle of Man became a tiny Viking kingdom.

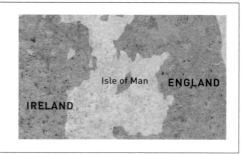

Bases in Ireland

Ireland was a wealthy country in the 700s CE. It was home to many fine monasteries, which were a target for Viking raiders. At first, the Vikings simply carried out raids, but gradually they set up camps in Ireland. Some of these camps developed into successful trading towns; Dublin, Wexford, Cork and Waterford all began as Viking camps.

The Irish people made repeated attempts to drive out the invaders. They had two great victories over the Vikings, first at the Battle of Tara in 980 CE, and later at the Battle of Clontarf in 1014 CE. After the Battle of Clontarf many Vikings were massacred, but not all of them were driven out of Ireland. The Irish rulers allowed some Vikings to stay because they brought valuable trade to their country.

A Viking settlement camp on the Irish coast

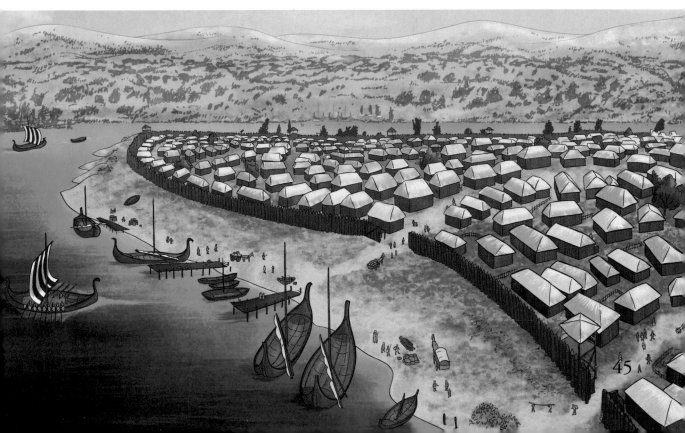

Vikings in Europe

By the 800s CE, Vikings were launching raids along the coast of western Europe, too. They set up camps near the coast and marched inland to loot and plunder major towns. Some raiders sailed south to reach the Mediterranean Sea. They launched attacks on Spain and Italy, and even raided places along the North African coast.

Vikings and Franks

In the Viking age, the countries that are now France, Germany, Belgium and the Netherlands all formed part of the enormous Frankish Empire. The empire was created in the 700s CE by the powerful ruler Charlemagne. During Charlemagne's lifetime, the Vikings had little success with their raids, but after his death in 814 CE, the Frankish lands were divided and fell into chaos. The Vikings took advantage of this weakness and invaded many major cities. Within fifty years, the cities of Nantes, Rouen, Paris, Hamburg, Ghent and Bordeaux were all looted and plundered.

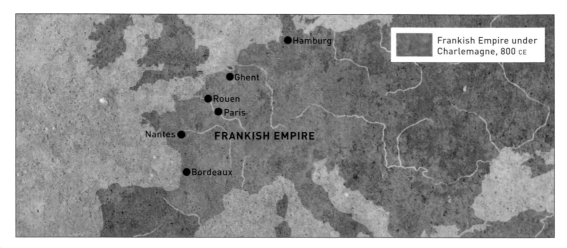

The kings fight back

By the end of the 800s CE, the European kings had strengthened their defences. They built castles and forts and trained efficient armies of mounted knights. In 885 CE, the Vikings launched an attack on the city of Paris, but the Frankish army resisted and fought back bravely. After ten months of fighting, the Vikings withdrew from Paris, although they continued raiding in other parts of France.

The gift of Normandy

Some Frankish kings took desperate steps to stop the raiding. They promised the Vikings money, and even land, in return for an end to the attacks. In 911 CE, King Charles the Simple gave the city of Rouen and its surrounding lands to a Viking leader called Rollo. In return, Rollo had to promise to be loyal to the king and become a Christian. Rollo's territory became known as *Terra Normannorum*, (the land of the Northmen). Later, it was known as the Duchy of Normandy.

Rollo the proud

Before Rollo could become ruler of Normandy, he had to pay homage to King Charles the Simple. This involved kneeling and kissing the king's foot. Rollo refused and ordered one of his warriors to take his place. The warrior lifted up the king's foot and sent him falling backwards!

Russia and Beyond

Some Vikings sailed east from their homelands. Tough warrior-merchants crossed the Baltic Sea and set up trading posts in Russia, close to rivers. During the winter, they raided the surrounding lands and gathered timber and furs. In spring, they rowed down the rivers, their boats laden with goods to trade.

Rurik and Oleg

The Russian settlements grew rapidly. By the 860s CE, a Viking leader called Rurik was ruling over a small kingdom surrounding the city of Novgorod. Rurik was succeeded by Oleg, who expanded his kingdom as far south as Kiev. This enormous territory was known as the principality of Kiev. The descendants of Oleg ruled the territory until 1598 CE.

In Russia and the East, the Vikings were known as the *Rus*, which means either 'the red-heads' or 'the rowers'. (This was the origin of the word 'Russians'.)

Rurik was the first in a long line of Viking rulers in Russia.

48

Difficult journeys

The Vikings travelled south for thousands of miles on the Russian rivers. Sometimes they had to make part of their journey overland. They carried the smaller boats over their heads. Large merchant ships were rolled on logs over the ground.

The city of Constantinople

Viking merchants from Russia travelled as far south as Constantinople, the capital of the Byzantine Empire (which was formed out of the old Roman Empire in the East). It was a busy meeting place for traders from all over Europe and Asia.

In 907 CE, the Vikings tried to invade Constantinople, but failed. They then tried to create good relations with the Byzantine emperors. In 988 CE, King Vladimir of Kiev sent highly trained Viking warriors to Emperor Basil II. These soldiers formed the emperor's bodyguard and became known as the Varangian Guard. Vladimir married the Byzantine Princess Anna, and became a Christian.

Arab lands

Viking raiders also attacked lands around the Caspian Sea. Some adventurous merchants reached as far as Baghdad (in Iraq) to trade goods for coins, spices, silks and jewellery.

Iceland, Greenland and North America

Some daring explorers sailed west from Scandinavia in search of new lands. Many ships were never seen again, but a few sailors returned with reports from the countries they had found. The Vikings set up colonies in the newly discovered lands, but not all their settlements were successful.

Voyages to Iceland

Around 860 CE, a Norwegian sailor called Naddod was blown off course and discovered the island of Iceland. Others followed him and in 874 CE, Ingólf Arnarson, a chieftain from Norway, brought settlers to live in Iceland.

Eric the Red in Greenland

Greenland was first discovered by Viking voyagers around 900 CE, but nobody landed there until Eric the Red about eighty years later. In 982 CE, Eric established a colony of settlers in southern Greenland. Life was very harsh for the settlers, but some Viking people stayed in Greenland until the 1400s CE.

Leif Ericsson in North America

Around the year 1000 CE, Leif Ericsson, one of the sons of Eric the Red, became the first European to reach North America. Leif and his crew spent the winter in an area that he named Vinland, which is probably present-day Newfoundland. Some adventurous Vikings began a new life in Vinland, but they were not welcomed by the Native Americans. After many battles, the settlers were forced to leave and return home.

Skraelings

The Vikings named the Native Americans 'skraelings'. This name may be linked to the Old Norse word for 'thin' or 'weak', or to the word for 'skin'. In the past, people thought skraeling meant a thin and wretched person. However, some experts now believe the skraelings got their name because they wore animal skins.

The Vikings faced fierce attacks from the Native American warriors.

The Last Vikings

After the death of King Cnut in 1035 CE (see page 43), his sons ruled England for another seven years. The Vikings then lost control of England and the Anglo-Saxons took over again. King Edward the Confessor ruled from 1042 CE to 1066 CE, but he died without an heir. Three men claimed the English throne after his death. One was an Anglo-Saxon, one was a true Viking and the other a descendant of Viking raiders.

Claiming the throne

William
of Normandy

The three rivals for the throne were Harold Godwinson, the Anglo-Saxon earl of Wessex, Harald Hardrada, the king of Norway, and William, Duke of Normandy. William was a direct descendant of the Viking leader Rollo (see page 47). Each man believed that he had the right to rule England, but the English nobles chose Harold Godwinson. Harald and William were furious and they both decided to launch invasions on England.

In early September 1066 CE, Harald Hardrada landed on the north-east coast of England. King Harold marched north to meet him. The English beat the Norwegians at the Battle of Stamford Bridge and Harald Hardrada was killed, but King Harold could not relax. Duke William had already landed on the south coast of England, and had built several forts to prepare for an English counter-attack. Harold led his army south, and on 14 October he was defeated at the Battle of Hastings. Harold died on the battlefield and William became the next king of England.

The end of the Viking age

Some people say the Viking age ended in 1066 CE. In fact, the raids continued in a few places for the next one hundred years, although they were much less frequent than before. The Christian kings of Norway, Sweden and Denmark established a firm control over their kingdoms and slowly the Viking way of life disappeared.

Duke William of Normandy defeated King Harold of England at the Battle of Hastings.

What the Vikings Did for Us

Even though the Vikings lived a thousand years ago, we can still see the mark they left on the world. Their descendants are spread throughout northern Europe and there is plenty of evidence of their influence on our lives today.

Great stories

The Vikings told brilliant stories of gods and giants, warriors, trolls and dragons. All these figures feature in modern books, films and games. Fantasy stories like Tolkien's *Lord of the Rings* include many elements from Viking culture. Tolkien even wrote about runes with secret meanings! Role-playing games like Warhammer are also inspired by the Old Norse legends. Their characters include gods, ogres and dwarfs, who play tricks on each other and wage savage battles – just like figures in Viking stories.

Days of the week

Some of our days of the week are named after Viking gods. Thursday comes from 'Thor's day' and Friday is 'Frey's day'. In Viking Britain, Odin became known as Woden. He gave his name to Wednesday, or 'Woden's day'.

Viking words

Some Viking words have become part of the English language. 'Earl', 'law', 'happy' and 'egg' are all Viking words. Many family names also have a Viking origin. Viking sons added the word 'son' to their father's name. So the son of Eric would have the last name 'Ericsson'. Modern surnames that end in 'son' began as Viking names.

Viking places

The Vikings established trading camps, such as York and Dublin, which later became great cities. They also left their mark on many smaller places. There are villages and towns with Viking names all over eastern and northern England. Place names ending in 'by', 'thorpe' and 'thwaite' all date back to Viking times. 'By' meant a village, 'thorpe' was a very small village, and 'thwaite' was a clearing in a forest.

The first parliaments

The Vikings were great law-makers. In their homelands, they gathered in open-air assemblies, called Things, to make their laws. This practice continued in some of the places where they settled, and the British parliament partly has its origins in the Viking Things. The link to the Vikings' outdoor assemblies is especially clear in the Isle of Man. The island's parliament, called the Tynwald, dates back to the time when it was ruled by Vikings. Even today, the Tynwald still follows the tradition of holding an annual outdoor meeting that everybody can attend.

Who's Who?

Ragnar Lodbrok (800s CE)

Ragnar is best known by his nickname 'Ragnar Hairy Breeches'. According to legend, his wife made him a pair of breeches (trousers) to resist dragon's breath. They were made from thick fur, boiled in tar and rolled in sand. Ragnar raided England but was captured by the king of Northumbria who, so the story goes, threw him into a pit of snakes.

Rollo the Ganger (c.860–932 CE)

Rollo's nickname means 'Rollo the walker', because he had to walk everywhere. He was so large that no horse could carry him! Rollo led the Vikings in a successful invasion of north-western France, and in 911 CE he was granted the right to rule this land by King Charles the Simple of France. Rollo's descendants became dukes of Normandy.

Eric Bloodaxe (died 954 CE)

Eric was the son of King Harald Finehair of Norway. He ruled Norway for a short time, but moved to England when his brother claimed the throne. Eric took part in raids on Scotland before becoming king of Northumbria, where he had two short reigns. In 954 CE, he was driven out of York and killed by an Anglo-Saxon army.

Eric the Red (c.950–1004 CE)

Eric the Red spent most of his youth in Iceland. After he killed two men, he was banished for three years. He sailed west and reached Greenland, where he spent the next three years exploring the country. In 982 CE, Eric returned to Iceland and the following year he sailed back to Greenland with around 500 settlers. Not all the settlers survived the journey and they struggled to stay alive in Greenland.

Sweyn Forkbeard (died 1014 CE)

Sweyn was the son of the Danish King Harald Blue-Tooth. He seized the throne from his father to become king of Denmark. In 1013 CE, he led a successful invasion of England. In the following year, Sweyn was crowned king of England, but he died just five weeks later.

Leif Ericsson (*c.* 970–1020 CE)

Leif was the second son of Eric the Red. He probably grew up in Greenland, and around 1000 CE he visited Norway. In Norway he was converted to Christianity by King Olaf Tryggvason who sent him to Greenland to convert the settlers. In one version of his life, he sailed off course on his voyage to Greenland and arrived in North America at a place he named Vinland. In another story, he heard of a land in the west from an Icelandic trader, and set off to find it. He spent the winter in Vinland and returned to Greenland the following year. His brother, Thorvald, made a second visit to Vinland.

Cnut Sweynsson (*c.*995–1035 CE)

Cnut Sweynsson is often known as Cnut the Great. He invaded England with his father, Sweyn Forkbeard, in 1013 and became King of England in 1016 CE. He followed his brother Harold as King of Denmark in 1018 CE, and conquered Norway in 1030 CE. During his reign, England was at peace and trade increased. A famous story tells how Cnut showed his followers that he could not control the sea: His courtiers placed his throne near the water's edge as the tide came in. Cnut commanded the tide to stop rising, but of course it did not.

Yaroslav the Wise (978–1054 CE)

Yaroslav was the son of a Viking ruler of Kiev. He fought his brothers to gain the throne and ruled Kiev from 1019 CE to 1054 CE. Yaroslav made Kiev into an important centre for learning. He encouraged trade with Constantinople and created a set of laws for the Russian people. Yaroslav made sure that Russia had links with the wider world. He married a Swedish princess, while his daughters married into the royal families of Norway, France and Hungary.

William of Normandy (*c.*1028–1087 CE)

William is usually known as 'William the Conqueror'. He was a descendant of Rollo the Ganger and the Viking dukes of Normandy and he became duke of Normandy in 1035 CE. When King Edward the Confessor died in 1066 CE William claimed that Edward had promised him the throne. He led an invasion, won the Battle of Hastings, and was crowned King William of England.

Timeline

600s/ 700s CE	Ancestors of the Vikings develop the ability to build longboats.
793 CE	Vikings raid the monastery of Lindisfarne, England.
794 CE	Vikings raid the monastery at Jarrow, England.
795 CE	Raids begin on the Scottish islands and in Ireland.
800 CE	Vikings set up camps in the Scottish islands.
814 CE	Charlemagne dies and his Frankish Empire falls into chaos.
830 CE	Raids on the British Isles and the Frankish Empire become more frequent. Swedish warrior-merchants settle in Russia.
841 CE	The Vikings set up a trading camp in Dublin, Ireland.
843 CE	Viking raiders stay in western France over the winter.
845 CE	The Vikings attack Paris. Their leader is Ragnar (possibly the man nicknamed 'Hairy Breeches').
850 CE	Danes stay in southern England over the winter.
859 CE	Vikings launch raids on Spain and the Mediterranean region.
860 CE	Rurik founds a Viking kingdom in Russia. Vikings reach Iceland.
865 CE	The Danish Great Army lands in England.
866 CE	The Great Army captures York in northern England.
870 CE	Harald Finehair unites much of Norway under his rule.
874 CE	Vikings settle in Iceland.
878 CE	King Alfred defeats the Danes at the Battle of Edington.
885 CE	Paris is attacked by Vikings, but holds out.

886 CE	Treaty between Alfred the Great and Guthrum, the Danish leader, sets the borders of lands that will become known as the Danelaw.
907 CE	Oleg, ruler of Kiev, sends a fleet to attack Constantinople.
911 CE	Lands in Normandy granted to the Norwegian Viking Rollo by the French ruler Charles the Simple.
930 CE	Establishment of Althing in Iceland, the world's oldest parliament.
954 CE	Death of Eric Bloodaxe. the last Viking ruler of York.
965 CE	King Harald Blue-Tooth of Denmark is converted to Christianity.
980 CE	The Irish defeat the Vikings at the Battle of Tara.
982 CE	Eric the Red starts to explore Greenland.
988 CE	Vladimir, ruler of Kiev, converts to Christianity.
990s CE	England and France pay money to the Vikings to stop their attacks.
c.1000 CE	Leif Ericsson and his crew reach North America.
1013 CE	Sweyn Forkbeard, king of Denmark, conquers England but dies soon afterwards.
1014 CE	The Irish defeat the Vikings at the Battle of Clontarf.
1016 CE	Cnut becomes king of England. He rules until 1035.
1042 CE	Edward the Confessor becomes king of England.
1047 CE	Harald Hardrada becomes king of Norway.
1066 CE	Edward the Confessor dies. Harold Godwinson is crowned king of England. King Harold defeats King Harald of Norway at the Battle of Stamford Bridge. Duke William of Normandy defeats King Harold at the Battle of Hastings. William of Normandy becomes king of England.
1100s CE	The Viking age comes to an end.

Glossary

ale beer

amber a yellowish substance made from hardened tree sap that is often made into beads

Anglo-Saxons the people who lived in England from around 410 CE to 1066 CE

archaeologist a person who learns about the past by digging up old objects and buildings

assembly a meeting of lots of people

banish to send someone away in disgrace

baptize to pour water over someone's head as a sign that they have become a Christian

campaign a series of events organized over a period of time in order to achieve or win something

cauldron a large metal cooking pot

CE dates after Christ's birth are described as CE (in the 'Common Era') e.g. 800 CE

ceremony actions, words and music to mark a special occasion. Ceremonies are often religious.

chainmail protective clothing for a soldier made from lots of metal rings linked together

chieftain a leader or ruler

civilization a well-organized society

colony a country or place that has been settled by people from another country

convert to change from one religion to another

culture	the way of life, traditions and ideas of a group of people
Danegeld	money paid to make the Danes go away
Danelaw	the area in England where the Danes lived in the 800s CE and 900s CE
descendant	someone from a later generation of a family
drinking horn	an animal horn used as a drinking container
empire	a group of countries with the same ruler
heir	someone who will inherit a title, money, land or property
inscription	letters or words that have been carved or specially written on an object
ivory	the substance elephants' and walruses' tusks are made of
javelin	a light metal spear
knorr	a ship used by merchants and settlers
longhouse	a long, rectangular house with one storey
loot	to steal
massacre	to kill large numbers of people
memorial stone	a stone carved in memory of someone
missionary	someone who tries to convert people to a new religion
monastery	a place where monks live and worship
pagan	someone who is not a Christian

Glossary

pewter   a type of metal that is dull grey in colour

plunder   to use violence to steal things

pole-lathe   a tool for turning wood into objects such as bowls

prow   the front part of a ship

rune   a letter used by the Vikings

sacrifice   to kill an animal or person as an offering to a god

Scandinavia   a region that includes Denmark, Norway, Sweden

settlement   a community of people who have gone to live in another country

settler   someone who goes to start a new life in another country

skald   a Viking poet. Some skalds played a harp

territory   land owned by a group of people and their ruler

Thing   a meeting held to make laws and discuss problems in the community

treaty   an agreement between one or more leaders

troll   a supernatural being in Viking legend. Trolls are often shown as short and hairy

tusk   long, curved and pointed tooth belonging to a walrus or an elephant

universe   everything in the world and beyond

Places to Visit

BRITAIN

Museums

Jorvik Viking Centre, York
The British Museum, London
The Hunterian Museum and Art Gallery, Glasgow
The National Museum of Scotland, Edinburgh
The Jewry Wall Museum, Leicester
Nottingham Castle Museum, Nottingham

Sites with remains of Viking buildings

Jarlshof, Shetland, Scotland
Brough of Birsay Island, Orkney, Scotland
The Braaid, Isle of Man

Sites with remains of Viking ship burials

Balladoole and Knock-e-Dooney, Isle of Man
Port an Eilean Mhòir, Ardnamurchan, Scotland
Scar, Sanday Island, Orkney, Scotland

SCANDINAVIA

Viking Ship Museum, Oslo, Norway
Museum of Cultural History, Oslo, Norway
Lofotr Viking Museum, Vestvågöy, Norway
Viking Ship Museum, Roskilde, Denmark
The Birka Museum, Stockholm, Sweden

CANADA

L'Anse aux Meadows, Newfoundland

Index